EXTRAVAGANT
LOVE

DEDICATION

This work is dedicated to every individual who has experienced horrific, abusive life circumstances, tormenting deeds, or tragic events that have left one questioning the very existence of God, or at minimum, His true nature.

ACKNOWLEDGMENTS

Extravagant Love is a project that I could never have completed on my own. From the first moments of inspiration to the finishing touches of this work, I have benefitted from the skill and expertise of dear friends, published authors, professional editors, and beloved family members.

I want to acknowledge the following for the many hours spent reviewing content and offering exceptional constructive feedback, encouragement, prayer, and support: Kriste Solomon, Lori Baxter, Lisa Woodward, Dan Helm, Chelsea Quenum, Deborah Mystikidas, and my husband, Tony Fournier.

For my church family in Stoke-on-Trent, United Kingdom, and the women who first asked me to write my biography, thank you.

Above all, my gratitude goes to my Savior, Jesus Christ, without Whom there would be no story to tell.

INTRODUCTION

Is God uncaring, uninvolved, and untrustworthy? Or is the eternal Almighty God a loving and engaged Father, merciful and kind beyond our human ability to fully comprehend?

I have come to know that His love is without limit or measure and that He seeks to lavish this upon me even more than I desire to experience it. He delights in exceeding all bounds and displaying His love in such elaborate ways that I am awestruck.

My prayer is that by the time you have finished reading my story, you will be convinced of His goodness and transformed by this unalterable truth: God *is* love.

What this God of love has done for me He longs to do for you.

> "Consider the kind of extravagant love the Father has lavished on us—He calls us children of God! It's true; we are His *beloved* children..."
>
> 1 John 3:1 (VOICE)

Chapter One

HE FOUND ME

"Gunfire! Oh, dear God, no!"

The loud blast of our .22 caliber hunting rifle was reverberating through the air. My heart beat wildly within my chest as I struggled to breathe.

"Is he alive? Did he discharge the bullet into the air again? Or is he dead?" Tormenting moments passed as my family and I waited to learn whether this was the latest incident of threats to self-harm, or if this time, my father had followed through with his plans to end his own life.

Out of the eerie silence that followed that devilish blast, we heard my father's quaking voice. "I'm okay. The gun went off accidentally."

The calendar dates of this traumatic experience, and so many others like it, are no longer stored in my memory. But one extraordinary date will never be forgotten.

July 14, 1973. I did not realize it then, but on that day, my life changed forever.

1

***

By the time I was born, the last of twelve children, several of my siblings had already left home to begin their own lives. Some had settled quite a distance from us and visited once a year or less. Others were a bit closer to home and visited more often. None were able to come and see us as frequently as my longing heart desired.

As a young teen, I could not comprehend why they had felt such a necessity or urgency to leave home. Why did they have to go? Had they gone to a better situation? Were they happy? Would they forget me?

But on this special day, the reverse was happening. One of my five brothers had arrived back home. He, too, had moved out of state shortly after high school graduation, and I missed him terribly. His visit broke the monotony of end-less, sweltering summer days.

I was overjoyed at how different he seemed from what I remembered. High school had afforded heartache and trial enough for him, after all, it was the seventies. The drug culture, poverty, racial and class tensions, and the boredom of living in a small town had entangled many of our classmates. Premature loss of life had been the outcome for more than one. Could these sad events paired with the loud arguments and physical altercations I had witnessed between him and my father be the reason he had left home at seventeen?

How surreal it all seemed seeing him exuding tremendous joy and peace. Focused and unrelenting, he had returned with the intent of sharing his newfound happiness with all of us. Happiness? Peace? Joy? Certainly these were welcomed, yet infrequent commodities in our home environment. All was well when there was sobriety, but our world rapidly morphed into misery and torment when alcohol was present.

"Let's find a quiet spot where we can talk, Irene." My brother, Bill, and I chose a room on the second floor of the farmhouse my family rented and sat for a few minutes of uninterrupted conversation.

He spoke enthusiastically of the experience that had effected such great change in his life. At first, it seemed like a fairy tale, simply too good to be true, but I had no reason to distrust his words. Truth be told, I envied him and dared to hope his story could be mine, as well. Minutes quickly passed as I listened to the simple explanation of the event which had led to his undeniable life transformation.

"Jesus came to bear the sins of all the world, mine and yours included, Irene, and to take the punishment for them. He offers, instead, the gift of eternal life in heaven—eternal happiness. All you need do is believe this, accept Him as your

3

personal Savior, and make Him the Lord of your life. I'm going to pray. You repeat what I say."

"Okay." I willingly and obediently followed his instructions. "Jesus, I believe You are the Son of God, and that You died on the cross for my sins. I repent now and ask You to come into my heart and be my Savior and the Lord of my life." When we finished, he exuberantly announced that I was now *saved*.

"Thanks for praying with me. Is that it?"

"Yes, that's all you need to do."

"Great. I will see you later."

Heading down the stairs, it seemed nothing had really changed; at least, I didn't feel any different. Regardless, I could no longer stay inside the house on that beautiful summer day. I needed to get back to practicing my gymnastics for cheerleading tryouts.

I was thirteen, and my pursuit of becoming a member of the cheerleading squad surpassed settling the matter of my eternal destiny. In fact, I had been quite oblivious to the existence of that need. After all, I went to church every time my family did. Church attendance seemed more than sufficient to satisfy any religious requirements for me to eventually access heaven.

July 14 was a marked day, but it would take me some time to fully realize the significance of what had transpired—or so I thought.

That following morning, while taking my first steps out the door to begin my farm chores, something caught me completely off guard. Feelings of peace and joy flooded over me at an overwhelming rate. To my amazement, the grass appeared unusually green and the sky the most brilliant blue. I felt light and so serene.

Am I floating, or are my feet still on the ground? I thought. *What has happened? What huge weight has lifted off of me?*

The presence of this foreign sensation enveloping my entire being could only be traced back to the simple prayer spoken the day before. Nothing else in my environment had changed and no other reasonable explanation could be found.

My eyes were open to the reality that something or someone had reached down from heaven into a dilapidated two-story farmhouse in Southern Illinois, directly into the heart of a clueless young girl, and I knew then that I would never again be the same.

These feelings of happiness, love, and peace seemed so new, yet strangely familiar. How could it be both? I then realized these feelings were what my brother had. It wasn't a fairy tale after all for nothing could have been more real.

Days passed and I continued to muse over my prayer of commitment to Jesus and the feelings so fresh in my entire being. I reflected on how our family attended church on most Sundays, how we read from the Bible, took communion, and prayed often. We believed in God, and in the death, burial, and resurrection of Jesus Christ, His Son. Still, this new deep level of connection with Jesus that I possessed was so powerful! It could only be described as entering into a very real and personal relationship with Him.

Prior to that day (and to the bold witness of my brother), I had not known that such closeness to Jesus was available. I had been raised to believe that it was unattainable unless you were the priest in a pulpit or perhaps a nun in a convent. Surely, they were the only ones who could know this level of connection with God.

Nevertheless, there I was beginning a deeply personal journey with Jesus and experiencing a yearning to grow in this newfound relationship.

Would everything change now? I wondered.

> "I was sought by those who did not ask for Me; I was found by those who did not seek Me…"

> Isaiah 65:1

Bill and Irene—July 1973.

Chapter Two

THE THINGS WHICH
ARE DESPISED

Has he come home? Did he have whiskey or just beer? Did I hide the rifle and the kitchen knives?

Fearing that my father would harm himself or the family when drunk, my siblings and I routinely hid anything that could be used as a weapon. Despite our best efforts to protect ourselves and each other, there were numerous occasions when tormenting situations still occurred within the confines of our family home.

"Quick. Get the screwdriver, the hammer, the ax if needed, and get that door open." Almost too frightened to react, one of my older brothers worked furiously to gain access to our parents' bedroom where my father had locked himself in and shot off the hunting rifle. Had he taken his own life *this* time?

How I longed and prayed for these terrifying events to never recur and for our home to be filled with a sense of safety, peace and happiness. From my earliest childhood memories, I questioned, *Why can't we just have a normal family life?*

Yet, this monster called alcoholism, with its favorite minions of violence, abuse, and mental torment, remained an unwelcome and constant resident. It seemed to overshadow the good experiences until they could hardly be found.

Tagged as "the family from the other side of the tracks," the ones people were embarrassed to be seen with, very little of my family's activities were hidden from the all-knowing eyes and ears of the residents in our small township and surrounding communities.

Like Otis, the fictional town drunk of Mayberry on the American TV sitcom *The Andy Griffith Show*, my father was well known by the local law enforcement officers and spent many nights in jail sobering up. Unlike Otis, whose antics resulted in harm to no one other than himself, my father's behavior while under the influence was guaranteed to cause harm to many and resulted in actions that would leave most, if not all, of our family members deeply wounded and potentially scarred for life.

Still, I found myself consumed with a longing that our neighbors, my school friends, and the community could see my father when he was not drinking. These were rare, yet good times when his true nature of kindness, gentleness, honesty, integrity, and diligent labors to provide and care for his family were plainly manifest.

Constantly, I would remind myself of the special times I had shared with my father. How delighted I was when the monthly social security disability check arrived in the mail, and I could, once again, ask my dad to buy a child's essential groceries, such as strawberry soda and the ingredients needed to make Rice Krispie treats. And he would just to make me, the baby of the family, happy. These were the simple, yet bonding moments that sustained me through miserable difficulties and would continue to sustain me through trials yet to come.

How is it possible that alcohol addiction can so alter the behavior of a person? How can someone normally so gentle and kind transform into an abuser? How can one who had experienced so much familial torment become a tormenter himself? Who would be able to break this generational pattern and offer protection and normalcy?

Physical, verbal, emotional, mental, and sexual abuse had been present in my grandparents' lives, and had found inroads to ravage every member of my family. How many more generations would be destroyed?

Though I knew my father loved us, he seemed incapable of stopping his own violent and abusive behavior. Nor was he able to protect us from other perpetrators.

This is not my father, I would reason. *My father loves us and truly wants the best for us… But who or what rules this home? Why does it have to be like this?*

In so many ways, our family was not unlike many others living in rural America and struggling to have the best life we could. Our Polish heritage had instilled in us an extraordinary work ethic, and prior to his receiving the diagnosis of a disabling heart condition, my father worked diligently to provide for us. Whether working in the steel or lumber industry, for the railroad, or on the farm, my father worked from the time he arose in the morning until dusk prohibited further labor.

We farmed wheat, corn, and soybeans in their seasons. We raised acres of garden vegetables which my mother industriously canned to sustain us through the winter. We sold what remained at our makeshift roadside stand. We worked from sunup to sundown, traded pigs and other farm animals with the neighbors, watched an hour of *Hee-Haw* together on our black-and-white television set, and went to bed. The next morning started the routine all over again.

Although we were often without daily necessities, I found myself longing and praying for the calendar days to change quickly. The first of the month meant the disability check would come in the mail, and the all-too-familiar cycle would start again. There would be a little money to use wisely or to squander away. Ironically, I longed for the middle of the month when the funds would be exhausted, even though I knew we would suffer until the next month began. Going without food was much easier to bear than the terrifying scenarios that often played out in our home.

Who would we need to protect tonight: my mom or another family member? Would my mom spend the night in the cold barn in her lightweight nightgown, hiding for fear of bodily harm? Would the table be overturned in the kitchen, and would I cower there watching physical fights between family members that I was completely powerless to stop? Would the block of wood swung at my brother's head kill him?

So often I questioned how many more times these scenes could be repeated before a member of my family was seriously hurt—or worse. Would my family and I always be locked in this prison of shame and violence? Would we forever be despised and left without hope?

> "For you see your calling, brethren, that not many wise according to the flesh, not many mighty, not many noble, *are called*. But God has chosen the foolish things of the world to put to shame the wise, and God has chosen the weak things of the world to put to shame

the things which are mighty; and the base things of the world and the things which are despised God has chosen, and the things which are not, to bring to nothing the things that are, that no flesh should glory in His presence."

1 Corinthians 1:26–29

My dad, Leo, on the farm.

Chapter Three

BEHOLD, ALL THINGS HAVE BECOME NEW

My years as a teenager were filled with as many questions as I had answers. Life seemed to be presenting two perspectives that were polar opposites. There were two worlds to choose from: the heavenly world my brother had introduced me to on that July day or the harsh earthly world I was living in.

From the moment I voiced that prayer, everything had changed on the inside. Of that, I was absolutely sure. Of my great need to understand how to survive in this surreal and painful daily environment, I was also sure.

"Where do I turn, Jesus?" I prayed, "Where do I find the answers?"

The reply to my desperate cries came immediately.

"When you seek Me with all your heart, you will find Me. As you read My Word, I will teach you and guide you."

Though these words were not audible, I knew beyond a shadow of a doubt that Jesus had spoken to me and answered my pleas for help. I had heard Him in my spirit.

Daily, I read the Bible and prayed. The words on the pages were alive, and they were instructing, comforting, and strengthening me. They were teaching me how to walk in the new things, in the ways of the kingdom of God and no longer in the kingdom of darkness.

I also found help by reflecting on the transformation my brother had experienced and by incessantly asking him many of my questions. He had gone ahead of me into this new world of walking with Jesus in a very personal and fully committed way, and had wonderful wisdom to share. We had grown up together and experienced the same agonies and disappointments, but now, we were experiencing the new things that the Bible speaks of—freedom from guilt and shame, peace, and unspeakable joy.

Though my brother had also been a victim of the routine mental and physical abuse in our home, he was now walking in peace of mind and newness of life. When I experienced doubts or questions about the reality of my new life, I reminded myself to look at the lasting fruit of his life's transformation.

Bill's personal testimony served as a stabilizing influence when my own doubts and questions arose. I had witnessed his life before, and was now witnessing his life after his complete surrender to Jesus Christ.

***

During his senior year of high school, he had begun to take on the common appearance of the seventies and had grown his hair long. On one occasion, I watched helplessly as my father, intoxicated and filled with rage, grabbed him by the back of his head and pulled out a large amount of hair. That was the evening he chose to leave home.

With nowhere to go, he walked the railroad tracks for ten miles to the outskirts of a nearby town and searched for a safe location to spend the night. A church had left their door open, so he went inside and attempted to sleep. The following morning, while wandering around the town trying to figure out what his next steps would be, he met a man he vaguely recognized—a minister who had spoken at an all-school assembly. This godly and compassionate man invited my brother into his home for safe lodging and to church the next morning.

Typical in appearance with its white clapboard siding and a cross mounted on top of its steeple, no one would have guessed the life-changing things that were taking place inside that small Baptist church. The guest speaker that Sunday was a missionary who engaged in the dangerous work of getting Bibles to Christians behind the Iron Curtain. He was passionately teaching from the Bible, the songs sung by the choir were touching the hearts of those in attendance, and the atmosphere was electric with a Holy Presence.

Bill testified that he began experiencing a heaviness in his heart regarding the things he knew he had done that were displeasing to God. Simultaneously, this conviction of sin was accompanied by a fantastic invitation to draw near to God and receive the free gift He was offering to all—the gift of forgiveness of all sins and eternal life in heaven.

With the popular gospel song "Just as I Am" playing in the background, he made his way out of the church pew and down to the altar to surrender his life to Jesus once and for all. Thus, he became the first one in our family to receive the unconditional love of God in this incredibly personal way. God, our Father, had rescued him from loneliness, distress, and homelessness.

After that glorious Sunday morning, he began traveling to nearby towns, working alongside the godly itinerant minister. Shortly after, he left Illinois to make Florida his new home. It was the days of revival, and Jesus People were multiplying everywhere. There were music bands outdoors, chapel times indoors, and street evangelism was prolific. It was from this new and exciting life in Florida that my brother had returned to visit with us that life-changing July.

***

Although I rejoiced greatly at his new life, happiness, and sense of purpose, my young mind still struggled to make sense of it all. Daily Bible reading and prayer, recalling Bill's testimony, and reminding myself of what I had experienced the day after praying with him kept me encouraged on my darkest days. Yet, I knew there had to be more. I knew I had changed on the inside and no one could take that away from me, but what would change the outside circumstances?

Would there always be this struggle and oppression inside my home? What did my future look like? Like my sisters and brothers before me, would I, too, have to leave home and my family at the first opportunity to find external peace and safety?

In order to survive my high school years, I resigned to do the only things I knew at that time. I prayed to God, my Heavenly Father, found solace and strength in reading the Bible, and spent as much time as possible with my Christian friends and their families.

I worked extra hard gaining an education, praying and hoping my future would hold something very different from what now encompassed me. Excelling academically did not come naturally for me, but I was determined to do my very best to make something of myself and overcome the canopy of shame that shrouded my home. Though small consolation, it meant the world to me to be named a member of the

National Honor Society; to have someone or some organization say I wasn't despised—at least, not in every way.

Following the advice of my high school guidance counselor, I chose a track of subjects that would prepare me to enter the secretarial world. Who could have known that Gregg Shorthand wouldn't be useful in just a few short years, or even typewriters for that matter? Nonetheless, this counsel helped me to establish a solid foundation upon which to build a satisfying and successful administrative career.

I could not see my future, but my Heavenly Father could. He knew He was directing me in preparation for an administrative career with an educational program in another state. A program where I would be richly blessed to use my hard and soft skills, serve the needs of children with sensory disabilities, and where I would establish wonderful lifelong friendships with my co-workers. His plans were to prosper me and to give me a future.

I still struggled at times to be free from the ever-present feelings of fear, depression, hatred, anger, and shame that often filtered out of our private home and into every part of my life. As a new Christian, surely there was more than this to the abundant life promised in Scripture. Surely the all-powerful love of God that had changed Bill and I could change all things and make them new, couldn't it?

"Therefore, if anyone *is* in Christ, *he is* a new creation; old things have passed away; behold, all things have become new."

2 Corinthians 5:17

Chapter Four

SETS THE SOLITARY

"Irene?"

"Here."

"Carol?"

"Here."

Roll call was being taken in homeroom. It was the first day of our freshman year in high school. Feeling a tap on my shoulder, I turned to investigate the face of a stranger who asked, "Are you Bill's sister?"

Startled, I answered her question with a question. "Yes, what of it?"

In our very rural community, elementary school had been first through eighth grade. With no transition period, I was launched into the frightening world of our local community's high school and was currently encountering my first unsuspected connection. Someone who knew my brother was sitting right behind me.

Carol had met my brother at the local Baptist church where he had answered the altar call and received Jesus as his

Savior. Wanting me to have Christian friends in high school, he had asked her to seek me out and befriend me. Carol wasted no time in doing just that. Soon, I was being introduced to another friend, Connie. We would become known as the "Christian trio" of our high school and would remain friends into our adult lives.

When life became too difficult in my own home, Carol or Connie would graciously invite me to spend the weekend with them, and their families soon became my own. Connie's mother, Lee, became my second mom. Love, acceptance, safety, and the most practical needs of food and shelter were provided repeatedly throughout the four years that followed. Lee and her husband, Russell, would often take in foster children and offer the same loving shelter to them.

These families became my refuge from the continuing troubles within the walls of my home. They were my little piece of heaven on Earth. Though not perfect, the examples of their lives filled me with hope that families could live harmoniously—that they could overcome obstacles as they relied upon Jesus for help and wisdom.

Thankful for good friends, safe places, and times of peace and provision, I wondered still when my own family circumstances would change for the better.

"God sets the solitary in families; He brings out those who are bound into prosperity; But the rebellious dwell in a dry *land*."

Psalm 68:6

Irene, Connie and Carol—the "Christian trio."

Chapter Five

PROMISE OF POWER

Typically, our high school years offer us a multitude of life lessons. Perhaps for me the most significant of all revolved around an assignment given in my freshman English class. We were to compose a topical essay on the most important event in our lives.

My encounter with Jesus over the past summer was fresh, vibrant, and without a doubt, the undisputed topic for my paper. Composing came so easily. Reading it publicly in the classroom was a different story.

As I read, praying the hearts and minds of my classmates would be touched by this wonderful news, the reactions began. Scanning the faces, it was unmistakable that one person in particular was becoming agitated, almost angry. This distress would be acted upon and a stream of vile verbal attacks would follow, and continue for the next four years.

Was it his particular assignment to make me miserable? To torment me? What had I done to deserve this? Without doubt, I had enough to deal with inside my own home. I didn't need his abuse, too.

I began searching through the Bible for the instructions on how to navigate this troubled pathway. Scripture verses seemed to leap off the page. Many spoke of loving your enemies and praying for those who say all manner of evil against you falsely for the sake of Jesus' name.

Desire as I did, I could not always find the depth of strength within myself to conduct my behavior in accord with such a high call. Beyond that, I began to wonder how I would find the strength to share my personal testimony of coming to know Jesus if this was going to be a common response. I was quickly learning a crucial life lesson—I needed power and strength much greater than my own.

One specific Bible verse absolutely intrigued me. It spoke of receiving a gift that would help me understand the Scriptures, overcome sin, and grant me the power to be His witness. This was exactly what I was looking for! Seeking this gift became my obsession for the next several months, and eventually, years.

According to the Scriptures, in the Book of Acts, this gift would answer the current needs and cries of my heart and fill me with a holy power that would enable me to continually testify of the goodness of God.

I soon learned that this gift was called "baptism in the Holy Spirit." I recalled that my brother had spoken to me of this and testified of receiving it himself, so I began to read not only the Bible, but books that contained stories of those whose lives had been changed by this heavenly endowment.

One author wrote his opinion of how to experience or receive this gift, while another author had a completely different idea. One person dogmatically believed it was a legitimate experience; another believed it was false, and even dangerous. Still another stated it was only for those who were alive during Bible times. How was a fourteen-year-old new believer in Jesus Christ to figure this out?

Carol and Connie had both experienced this, and they seemed fine and normal. Actually, they seemed to have something a little beyond normal. Was this the power spoken of in the Bible? Why were they bold to tell others about Jesus? Why were they succeeding in loving their enemies? And why did they have such deep, unshakable joy? How I wanted that unquenchable joy to invade my home life and my school life!

Putting aside the conflicting opinions, I went back to my Bible for guidance. What did Jesus say about this gift? I found that answer quickly while reading through the Gospel of Luke.

Jesus had told His first disciples that the Heavenly Father would not give them anything that would harm them. Rather,

He commanded them to not leave Jerusalem until they had experienced the fulfillment of His promise that He Himself would send them the Holy Spirit with power. Taking Jesus' words at face value, I became convinced that this promise was for me, too.

Then and there, I determined that I had to take the risk. I locked myself in a room inside our rented house, determined to pray and not come out until I had received this gift from above. Hours later, I came out of the room unchanged. My times of seeking were repeated over and over again as the months and years went by. Finally, I concluded (in error) that my seeking was in vain, and this gift really wasn't for everybody. Still, I could not shake the longing and deep desire to possess this much-needed strength.

Perhaps it was my observation of Carol and Connie—of how they lived what seemed to be a more victorious life—that kept me from giving up all hope and pursuit. Or perhaps it was the memory of my brother's testimony of what he had experienced when he received this gift. If God had given them His Holy Spirit, then why would He not do the same for me?

It would be my senior year of high school before the topic came up again.

***

My girlfriends and I had been invited to a youth meeting. The guest speakers included a ministry team from a Bible college in Seattle, Washington. How odd it seemed that they had found their way to our tiny rural community.

One of the guest speakers at the meeting asked, "Who in this room has not yet been filled with the Holy Spirit?"

I remember thinking, *I'm not raising my hand. I've asked a million times already, and for some reason, God doesn't seem to want me to have this.*

Prodded by my faithful friends, and with great reluctance, my hand went up in the air and I was invited to take the seat in the middle of the prayer circle. As the group joined hands and began praying loudly in both English and in what sounded like foreign languages, they asked that I might now receive this promised gift. Frightened by the volume and intensity of their prayers, and more disappointed than ever, I left the circle unchanged—or so I thought.

Weeks passed and a new invitation came from Connie.

"Do you want to go to a fellowship this Saturday night? It's a weekly meeting hosted by a charismatic Catholic couple who love helping high school and college-aged students grow in their relationships with Jesus."

"Sure, that sounds great," I agreed. After all, these meetings got me out of my family's house for the weekend and into the coveted, safe, and healthy environment of Connie's home.

As the meeting in this lovely couple's house began to wind down, the host asked us to break up into small groups and pray for each other. That was scary. No one in my group seemed to want to pray, and I grew impatient.

"Fine! I'll do it."

As I began to open my mouth to pray, a strange language poured out. Sensations of great warmth and feelings of unadulterated joy flooded my entire being. What was this? Depression was lifting, anger was dissipating, and bitterness could no longer find a place to reside within me. I could see a dark shroud being carried away from me. I was buoyant as though floating in the clouds. This marvelous, multilayered experience wasn't stopping and, frankly, I didn't want it to.

I had planned to pray the way I always did, in English. My Heavenly Father evidently had a different idea for that exact moment in time. It seemed He had snuck up on me when I was least expecting it. After four years of on-and-off seeking, He chose *that* moment to reveal to me that He had both heard and answered the cries and longings of my heart to receive the baptism in His Holy Spirit. Something had happened when the Seattle ministry team prayed for me in that uncomfortable setting weeks prior.

That evening, Carol and Connie were in a different prayer group than me, so I could hardly wait to get to Connie's house to share my excitement with her. Now that I had received this new prayer language, I could hardly contain my joy and desperately hoped that Connie and I could continue to pray together.

"Connie, guess what happened?!"

"It's obvious, Irene. You have received the baptism in the Holy Spirit!"

Oh, how I wanted that evening to never end! "Please, dear God," I prayed. "Make this heavenly joy and buoyancy stick. Don't let the depression, anger, or shame come back. They were so overpowering. I want to be ruled by Your Spirit, not by my own strength that fails, not by these feelings that have been my dreaded companions these sixteen years, nor by the yet unchanged external circumstances of my daily life."

Unspeakable joy, peace that passed understanding, boldness that rose within, assurance that I was beloved of God—these were the phenomenal things I now sensed inside. Jesus' words, recorded in the Gospel of John chapter 14 began echoing in my ears and in my heart.

> "If you love Me, keep My commandments.
> And I will pray the Father, and He will give
> you another Helper, that He may abide with
> you forever—the Spirit of truth, whom the
> world cannot receive, because it neither sees
> Him nor knows Him; but you know Him,

for He dwells with you and will be in you. I will not leave you orphans; I will come to you...But the Helper, the Holy Spirit, whom the Father will send in My name, He will teach you all things, and bring to your remembrance all things that I said to you. Peace I leave with you, My peace I give to you; not as the world gives do I give to you. Let not your heart be troubled, neither let it be afraid."

John 14:15–18, 26–27

Suddenly and quite unexpectedly, as He did on that day in July, God's unconditional love had, once again, burst into my life with such magnitude and such depth that it took my breath away! In the boondocks, in that beautiful little farmhouse owned by a caring and sacrificial couple and surrounded by cornfields, Jesus had found me. True to His Word, He had fulfilled so many of His promises, and they were for me after all!

From that time forward, I knew something deep within me had changed permanently. A profound deliverance and healing from grief and shame had transpired. Along with depression, they had all been displaced, and I had received the promised Helper, the Holy Spirit of God, indwelling me and filling me to capacity with righteousness, peace, and exquisite joy.

> "But you shall receive power when the Holy
> Spirit has come upon you; and you shall be
> witnesses to Me in Jerusalem, and in all Judea
> and Samaria, and to the end of the earth."
>
> Acts 1:8

Chapter Six

IGNORANT NO LONGER

Puzzled, I sat in the Sunday morning service of a small church in Pinckneyville, Illinois, taking it all in. My mind was whirling with excitement and intrigue. Ministering from the pulpit in place of the one pastor I expected would be preaching, was a group of men and women much closer to my own age.

Interspersing Bible quotations, testimonies, and songs, they functioned as a well-practiced team. This was different. Who were they? How did they find this small town with a population of 2,500? Some of the faces looked familiar, and I realized they were part of the outreach group I had met; those who had encircled and prayed for me in that earlier home gathering.

"You, wearing the dark-blue dress, three rows from the back," a woman from behind the pulpit suddenly said. "You have a heart condition, and the Lord Jesus is healing that right now."

Who's wearing a dark blue dress? Does she really have a heart condition? How would this woman, this stranger at the front of the church, know that? I wondered. *How could she be so bold to speak it out for all to hear? Moreover, how could she possess and speak out with such great faith that Jesus was miraculously healing someone just a few pews away from me?*

I had experienced receiving the gift of eternal life through Jesus. I had sought after and finally received the promised baptism in the Holy Spirit. Without even asking, I had been wonderfully released from the death grip of depression, anger, bitterness, and shame. Now, someone was drawing back the curtain and letting me look into the next scenes of this life-long adventure called the Christian life. Entering stage right were the spiritual gifts I had read about in the Bible in the Book of 1 Corinthians chapter 12.

For the first time, I was witnessing the demonstration of the gifts of healings or perhaps the working of miracles. At minimum, this was a powerful example of the word of knowledge in operation, confirmed by the fact that the blue-dress wearer did, indeed, have a heart issue and did receive divine healing of it.

Could it be that beyond having my own life trans-formed, I, too, could be a part of someone else's life changing for the better? If this stranger can know these things and demonstrate such faith and boldness to help others, if she can operate in these spiritual gifts, can I do that, as well?

With the conclusion of the meeting, the team members began introducing themselves to those who lingered. Curiosity overcame me, and I had to ask: how had they come to be there? And how did they learn to minister in such a personal and life-changing way?

Soon, the testimony was shared of two of the team members, young men who had been involved in drugs in a small town only a few miles away from my home. Having become Christians, being divinely set free from addictions to drugs and alcohol, and now enrolled in a Bible college in Seattle, these two men had played a part in facilitating this outreach team by returning to the place of their roots.

Afterward, I learned that others in the neighboring town of Sparta were also enrolled at the same college. How encouraging to see and know firsthand that God's love could reach into farmhouses, tiny churches, and rural communities too small to be noticed by others.

High school graduation was only months away. Where would I go to college? Would I go to a Bible college? From the moment I began my walk and life with Jesus, I sensed deep within that I wanted to serve Him and to be in ministry. Could a woman do that? Apparently so, since I'd just witnessed several women ministering from the pulpit.

I was compelled to seek out a specific team member, a woman named Susan with the kindest face I had ever seen. I asked her to tell me more about the college she was attending, and as she did, I could barely contain my enthusiasm. But there was one more question I had to ask her.

How could I satisfy the seemingly contradictory Scriptures that kept me from making a definite decision about my future? One Bible verse told me to honor my parents and obey them in all things, while others told me to seek first the kingdom of God and His righteousness, and to love and obey God above everyone and everything else. I wanted to attend Bible college in obedience to the latter and to prepare to be in ministry, but my parents' disapproval and fear of anything outside the realm of their religious faith convinced me that they would be opposed to me attending a Christian Bible college.

"How do I choose?" I asked her. "I am going to end up disappointing someone, and that breaks my heart."

Amazingly enough, Susan had faced the very same personal dilemma. She took time to carefully explain how this had been resolved for her. As she had studied more of the Bible, she had come to understand that, oftentimes, many people mentioned in Scripture dealt with this issue. The answer was always the same—God's authority trumps all.

"We are commanded to obey our parents just as we are commanded to obey others who are in authority over us," Susan told me. "But when they instruct us to do something contrary to what is clearly directed in God's written Word, or they forbid us from doing something God clearly commands in that Word, then we must submit to His instruction and authority above theirs. God is the supreme and highest authority, and all are subordinate to Him."

Still not completely convinced and feeling more nervous than ever, I knew I needed this revelation from the Bible to be personally confirmed to me before I could make it a part of my foundation for decision making, especially life-altering decisions.

Susan directed me to Acts 4:17-20. The prior chapter and the other verses leading up to these explained how two of the early apostles of Jesus, Peter and John, were boldly proclaiming throughout the City of Jerusalem the good news of salvation through the name of Jesus. Additionally, while Peter and John ministered in Jesus' name, a man born lame at birth was miraculously healed. Sadly, the authorities, priests, rulers, elders, and scribes were upset by their preaching and this testimony of healing. They had Peter and John arrested. In verses 17 and 18, they threatened them and commanded them to stop preaching in Jesus' name.

This dilemma was a good example of my own struggle between two seemingly opposing voices. Peter and John had walked with Jesus, and they had been present when He commanded them to go and make disciples of all nations and teach them the things He had taught them. Which authority did they obey? Verses 19 and 20 reveal their response, "But Peter and John answered and said to them, whether it is right in the sight of God to listen to you more than to God, you judge. For we cannot but speak the things which we have seen and heard."

These verses answered the remaining questions and concerns for me, as well. Like them, I learned that in these unique circumstances in which two contrary voices were speaking, I had to listen to God above listening to men, even men and women in proper authority over me, such as my parents.

Now, settled by these Scriptures, I experienced a deeply longed-for liberty that enabled me to make the decisions necessary to begin planning the next phase of my marvelous journey with Jesus.

A sweet bonus to this weighty process was Susan's testimony that although her parents had, at first, objected to her plans, they were now attending the very same Bible College! Carol and Connie were making similar plans. Within weeks of graduating, we began our new adventure: traveling to Seattle together.

But one thing had to be done before I could leave… I had to tell my parents of my plans to move out of state and attend a Christian Bible college.

"Precious Lord Jesus, how do I do that?" I prayed. "Please prepare their hearts, and please give me Your wisdom to know what to say and how to say it."

> "But the manifestation of the Spirit is given to each one for the profit *of all*: for to one is given the word of wisdom through the Spirit, to another the word of knowledge through the same Spirit, to another faith by the same Spirit, to another gifts of healings by the same Spirit, to another the working of miracles, to another prophecy, to another discerning of spirits, to another *different* kinds of tongues, to another the interpretation of tongues."
>
> 1 Corinthians 12:7–10

Chapter Seven

FORSAKEN,
YET CARED FOR

"Mom, I need to let you know that I will be leaving soon. I'll be moving to Seattle to attend Bible college."

My mother's face filled with worry. Tears ran down her cheeks as she responded softly, "Your dad isn't going to like that."

"I know, mom, but I have to go."

Navigating through this straightforward conversation with my mother was bittersweet, but uneventful; however, discussing my move with my father did not go over as well. Traditions, firmly held beliefs, and fear fueled his intensely negative response to my announcement.

"You can go, but don't ever come back home. You are not my daughter anymore."

Somewhere along the line, *Catholic* and *Christian* had become powerfully opposing terms for my parents. Attendance at any church, prayer meeting, fellowship, or religious function that did not originate with or bear the approval of the Roman Catholic Church was forbidden and frightening to them.

Vividly, I recalled how well this had been exemplified on a particular Sunday morning several years prior. In my naivety, I had agreed to visit the local Pentecostal church with two of my eighth-grade classmates. Before the blue church bus, which had transported me to and from the church service, had even left our driveway, the verbal attack began.

"What do you think you're doing?!" my dad lashed out, his face contorted in anger and profound confusion. "You're Catholic! We don't go to other churches! If we do not remain faithful Catholics, we go to hell!"

Those foreboding words were, again, ringing in my ears.

Fear of my being so far away from home and the deeper fear of me losing my salvation and being damned to hell forever were the underlying foundation for my father's response. Though I knew these motivating factors were present, they could not, in and of themselves, stop the pain and the rejection I was experiencing in that moment. My earthly father had cast me off. I had been forsaken and cut out of the family forever. In choosing to follow Jesus fully, this was not a cost I had expected to pay.

During the previous four years, I had managed to secretly attend Christian functions, sneaking out for this Bible study, that prayer gathering, or the occasional Sunday morning church service with Carol or Connie. Now, everything was being forced out into the open. I had to pack my meager belongings, give notice at my after-school job, and arrange travel to Seattle.

Would I have to sneak away from home again, this time for good? Would I not be able to say goodbye to my family for fear that they would try to stop me? How would this transition happen without me hurting my parents more than they were already hurting? "God, grant me the grace and strength to bear my own emotional pain as well," I prayed.

***

Weeks passed. Before we knew it, the day we were scheduled to leave Illinois and begin our five-day road trip was upon us. Carol, Connie, and I, along with two others, would travel by car and van.

I attempted additional conversations with my parents to advise them that the time was drawing near and I would soon be leaving. To my dismay, it seemed everything kept pointing to the fact that I would need to depart in a covert way. I devised a plan wherein one of my brothers would drop me off at work before heading to his job at the local sawmill. The getaway vehicles would be waiting for me there.

Everything I owned was placed into one suitcase and stashed in the trunk of my brother's car. With two hundred dollars in my wallet, I was embarking on this exciting (although terrifying) new phase of my life.

Covering all bases, one of my traveling companions had penned a note saying that I was leaving of my own free will and requested that I sign it. Crossing the state line at age seventeen meant that I could be labeled a runaway and my parents could legally bring me back home. We didn't want anyone to be accused of kidnapping, and we certainly didn't need to add more difficulty to our situation.

The day finally came; the day I would leave for Seattle.

I hugged my brother who thought he was just dropping me off for work like he did every day, said the one goodbye I could say face-to-face, and asked him to relay this message to the rest of our family: "Please say goodbye to mom and dad for me, and tell them I love them." Turning to go, the flow of tears began.

How I wished things were happening in a different fashion. Not being able to personally say goodbye to my parents and siblings who remained at home was gut-wrenching. Would I ever be able to stop crying? Certainly not during the next five days of our journey.

Though I did not know it then, and though it would be a few months in coming, I was about to encounter the love of

God in such a powerful way that these recently accumulated feelings of abandonment, rejection, and grief would be significantly lifted from me. In time, complete healing would come.

Intense loneliness and sadness overwhelmed me during our travel from southern Illinois to Seattle. Nevertheless, God was going ahead of me, preparing to set me into an extensive loving family. This family numbered in the hundreds—my fellow Bible college students. He would take care of me just as He had promised in His Word, and the feelings of being forsaken by my earthly father were about to be overcome by the comfort of my Father in heaven.

> "When my father and my mother forsake me,
> then the LORD will take care of me."
>
> Psalm 27:10

Chapter Eight

LEAD ME TO THE ROCK

Lawrence, Kansas will forever be etched into my memory. We were only a day or two into our cross-country road trip when the transmission of our car began to fail. The estimated repair cost was $1,000.

As our small band of travelers looked at each other, we wondered how this obstacle would be overcome. All of our money pooled together barely totaled the required amount; we would have nothing left to help us get settled when we reached our destination. To the mechanic's astonishment, we informed him that we could not afford to have the car repaired and would be retrieving it from the garage in its impaired state.

"Let's pray." We laid our hands directly on the dashboard as an act of faith, and in the name of Jesus, we commanded the car to function properly. Bewildered, the mechanic watched as we drove away in what he knew to be a car that could no longer shift gears. Not only did we travel thousands of miles, cross mountain passes, and reach Seattle with this vehicle in running order, but the owner drove it for the next several years, never replacing the transmission!

Outside of the Bible, examples of God miraculously providing things such as food, rain, shelter, and safety from storms, I had never personally witnessed God demonstrating His love in such a practical and pragmatic way before. Truly, this was an extraordinary thing! This miracle was merely a prelude to the many miracles and praiseworthy things that I was about to witness and experience in the years to come.

Though thrilled about the car, I could not fully cap what seemed to be an endless well of tears regarding the grievous manner of separation from my family.

***

With eyes swollen and red, I stepped out of the car and onto the driveway of the Bible college campus. "Were we really here? How was this all going to turn out? Would my parents eventually be able to understand my decision? Would there ever be reconciliation and healing?"

The first level of answers to my unspoken questions came shortly after our arrival. Prior to the start of a particular Sunday evening church service, I clearly recall kneeling in prayer, arms crossed with my head resting on them on the seat of my chair. Tears were flowing again as I was desperately missing my family. Suddenly, as clearly as an audible voice speaking into my ears, I heard, *"When your father and mother forsake you, I will take you up."*

No longer aware of my natural surroundings, I began experiencing what by this time had become a familiar sensation—a great warmth settling over me. God's presence had drawn near as it had months prior when I'd received the baptism in the Holy Spirit. Grief, broken-heartedness, and disappointment were all being divinely removed.

How does He do that? I wondered. Joy seemed to enter every part of my inner being. In this realm of His presence, I could see myself being held and comforted by my Heavenly Father. *He's right here. He's reassuring me that all is well. He has taken me up and not forgotten me. He is so worthy of my trust.*

I wasn't expecting that when I knelt down. Jesus was becoming my best friend and confidant, the one to Whom I could pour out the depths of my soul. He was revealing Himself to me as one highly approachable and very willing to engage in real-life communion and interaction. I was also beginning to become familiar with the nature of the Lord— suddenly He comes and everything changes.

Every day of attendance at the Bible training center, I was learning how He desired to have a relationship with me even more than I desired to have a relationship with Him. He had loved me first from the moment He created me. My response could be none other than to yield to that love and to offer my love in return.

In my times of emotional turbulence, He had shown Himself to be the rock, the stable one that would not be moved by any assault. He had lifted me to that higher place with Him when I was overwhelmed. He had given me the garment of praise for the spirit of heaviness.

What was next in this great adventure?

> "From the end of the earth I will cry to You, when my heart is overwhelmed; lead me to the rock that is higher than I. For You have been a shelter for me, a strong tower from the enemy. I will abide in Your tabernacle forever; I will trust in the shelter of Your wings."
>
> Psalm 61:2–4

Chapter Nine

MY SHELTER AND MY STRENGTH

After my departure from home in the summer of 1977, communication with my family was pursued cautiously. I did not know what to expect after such an unceremonious parting, but I knew I had to keep a bridge of hope for restoration in place. When and how that bridge would be crossed remained to be seen. Human will and personal choices were involved. For my part, I knew my choice was to maintain faith, despite how things appeared, and to maintain a willingness to participate in the divine healing process.

My earthly father had disowned me, but I could not disown him nor forget my mother and siblings I had left behind. Everything I was learning and experiencing at Bible college filled me with faith and great hope that our relationships could be fully repaired. If the Lord was healing my broken heart, delivering me from the pain of rejection and abuse, and showering me with His unconditional love, would He not do this for them, as well?

How I longed for my mother to experience the warmth of our Heavenly Father's love that I had encountered so powerfully and was now experiencing daily. My continual prayer for her was that she be rescued from the damaging emotional torment and physical abuse she had endured year after year. I desired to see my three brothers still living at home know more than mere survival. I prayed that somehow I could become a blessing to them and help them see that life held so much more for them. Like my brother Bill had been for me, I wanted to be an agent of change and a bearer of hope for all of my family remaining in Illinois.

With this motivation, and hoping against hope, I timidly asked my father if I could come visit during the summer. His answer was a surprising "yes." Still feeling nervous about the decision, I began making plans to fly home to Illinois.

My summer visits were two-fold in purpose: to be reconciled to my family and to earn wages for the next year's tuition. Saving money to pay for tuition was much easier if I did not have dormitory rent to pay.

My high school secretarial training, along with experience of part-time jobs while a junior and senior in high school, made it easy for me to obtain clerical work in our County Clerk's office and for the local Farm Bureau branch in Pinckneyville.

Shortly after my arrival home in the summer of 1978, I realized that although not all of my choices had been pleasant or easy, they were absolutely necessary. Especially the simple, but hard choice to not allow unforgiveness and bitterness to consume me. The commandment of God to *forgive others as I have forgiven you* resounded loudly in my thoughts. Jesus was teaching me that I could not afford to allow a destructive root of bitterness to grow up in me. I needed to be obedient to His instruction to walk in peace, in holiness, and to remember the great grace He had already shown me. He wanted my family to know that great grace, as well!

That first summer, I did not want to acknowledge it, but the ever-present monsters of alcoholism, violence, verbal abuse, and emotional abuse had not been conquered, although perhaps they had slightly lessened in their intensity. During those months at home, I would often be the object of hours of hateful words spoken under their influence.

Everything came to critical mass one noteworthy summer evening. Replete with verbal abuse ignited by alcohol, I felt I could not stay in the situation one more moment. It was late afternoon, and I knew it would soon be dark, but I packed my one suitcase and walked out the front door without a backward glance. I remember thinking to myself that if I could not escape my living environment, I was literally going to have a nervous breakdown, but what could I do? I had not been home long enough to work and save the necessary money for fall tuition or for my plane fare back to Seattle.

I reached a majestic-looking walnut tree I loved about a mile down our country lane road, sat down on my suitcase under its great branches, and cried out to the Lord, "What am I going to do, Jesus?! I can't get back to Seattle yet, and I'm not strong enough to take this anymore. I'm wearing down and I feel that I will mentally snap!"

Within the half-hour, my father found me. "I'm sorry," he apologized. "I didn't mean to say those things. Please come back home; it will be dark soon."

I listened in astonishment, almost unbelief, as he apologized. My face drained of all color as I observed that he was divinely made sober, and that for the first time in my life, I was actually hearing my father ask me to forgive him for his abusive behavior. These two miracles were nothing short of divine intervention!

Jesus had answered my prayers quickly and had sovereignly touched my father's heart. I could see that for perhaps the first time, he was visibly shaken by the harsh reality and consequences of his actions, the eminent possibility of me leaving forever, and my near emotional breakdown.

The following seconds were swallowed up with nonstop, unspoken questions. *Is this how it happened? Is this why my mom suffered three nervous breakdowns? Is this why my brothers and sisters all left home in great haste? Were they escaping this inevitable outcome? Was the home in which we lived so overtaken by dark forces that we all needed deliverance and rescue?*

With my thoughts still in a flurry and with some degree of hesitation, I did return to the house with him. That a work had begun in him was undeniable. That there was so much more to be done was also undeniable. How would my Heavenly Father sort this out and make it right for all of us?

For the remainder of that infamous summer, the verbal assaults continued, but were minimized in impact as I prayed. They were muted at times by an unseen, but very much felt spiritual shield around me.

At the first indication that a verbal assault was about to begin, I would cry out to Jesus to help me, praying in English and in the unknown tongue or language I had received the night I had been baptized in the Holy Spirit. How grateful I was for that powerful aid!

Anchored on a particular set of scripture passages in Romans chapter 8 and a verse in the Book of Jude that revealed the powerful benefits of praying in this way to build up my strength, I pressed in and persevered through the remaining summer days at home. Though I was only able to process it at a beginner's level, I was learning firsthand what it meant to be involved in spiritual warfare. The enemy I was struggling against was not a human being of flesh and blood, but an unseen force of darkness.

By allowing the Spirit of God to pray through me as Romans chapter 8 explains, my own limited understanding of how or what to pray was bypassed. I had unshakable assurance that I was praying the express will of God. Consequently, I possessed the faith that my Heavenly Father would both hear and answer me.

This prayer strategy provided overcoming strength time and time again.

Indeed, this powerful chapter of the Bible was becoming a guidepost and a pillar upon which I would lean throughout my life. I had learned that the Holy Spirit helped in my weaknesses when I did not know what I should pray or even how I should pray. I experienced firsthand how He Himself prays for me, uttering things which cannot be articulated with natural and limited understanding. How marvelous was the revelation that He searches the hearts and knows how to plead my case and make intercession for me that is in complete agreement and alignment with the will of God.

During this season of my life, I was also experientially learning that not only was the Holy Spirit given to lead and guide me into all truth, but He really was my Helper and my Advocate, as well. And He was praying perfect prayers through me when I was unable to formulate the right thoughts.

Still, wisdom seemed to dictate that I begin to plan differently and not subject myself to this type of summer-break situation again. Until there was complete change, my visits home needed to be much, much shorter.

This internal prompting to trim down the length of my visits was cemented by my first supernatural dream. I had read about dreams given to Joseph, Daniel, and many others in the Bible, but it had not occurred to me that God might want to communicate with me through that method also.

By that time, I was becoming familiar with hearing His voice. I knew I had felt His presence. I had on many occasions experienced the sensations of warmth and peace that assured me He was near, but the reality of hearing from heaven in a dream was not yet something I had encountered.

One specific evening, I tossed restlessly on my daybed. It was one of three set up in the living room of our single-wide mobile home housing six adults. Two of my brothers slept on the other makeshift beds while my oldest brother living at home and my parents slept in the two bedrooms at either end of the mobile home. Finally, I drifted off to sleep and into a dream.

As though I had stepped inside a television and was playing a part in a movie based on the true story of my family life, the scenes and dialogue began to unfold. There were no other visible actors in this movie, yet I knew I could have conversations that would be heard.

As the dream began, I saw myself in my same location, on the daybed trying to sleep, but very much awake—awake and praying. I had seen a snake inside our dwelling.

"Is that an anaconda?" I queried. "It's the largest serpent I have ever seen. Why is it here?"

I heard no audible reply, but instantly knew it had been given the right to dwell there. "Jesus, what do I do? How do I make it leave?"

"Pray. Take authority over it and command it to depart."

I looked into its human-like eyes and spoke, "In Jesus' name, serpent, you must leave." After a purposeful, nonchalant stare, but no further resistance, it left. This seemed too easy and I began to wonder where it had gone.

As the dream scene changed, I found myself in the stand-alone garage on our property. I looked up to see the snake casually sprawled over the open timbers of the ceiling. Perplexed, I began to question the Lord. "Jesus, I don't understand. It didn't go away; it simply relocated. Will it try to come back inside our home?"

As clearly as though He were standing right in front of me, I heard His reply. *"Yes. If there remains an open door, it will have some access. But I have heard your prayers for deliverance* and reprieve, and you will taste the fruit of this level of victory. In time, the victory shall be complete."

Whether awakened by the uncomfortableness of a muggy August night in the Midwest, or simply because the dream had concluded, I sat upright and alert. My surroundings had not changed; everything was exactly as it had been before I drifted off to sleep.

That was a really weird dream, I thought, *Should I talk about it with anyone, or keep it to myself? What did it all mean?*

The full understanding would take years to come, as would the promised total victory, but one thing was certain: the dream was symbolic of the bondage of alcoholism and other addictions tormenting my father, and my prayers were making a difference in those bondages being broken. The serpent's choke hold had been weakened, its boundaries had been drawn, and eventually, it would meet its final end.

That summer of 1979 was truly unusual and, at times, very unpleasant. Nonetheless, I was learning more than one lifelong lesson in this season of testing. Jesus was faithfully proving to be my strength and my shelter in every circumstance of life. Through Him, being hidden in Him, I was protected and I was kept.

Grateful for this divine work within me, and sensing my spiritual roots were going down deeply like those of an oak tree, I still found myself longing for more. More restoration.

More healing. The recovery of what had been stolen away from my family members remained a primary pursuit. I desperately yearned for longstanding bondages and hurtful patterns to be broken.

Because the normal safety parameters for a family unit had been destroyed or grossly damaged through addictions, my mother, my siblings, and I were all subjected to varying types and levels of abuse. We were all affected differently, and we were all coping differently.

Knowing God's unconditional love could change things, and knowing that nothing was impossible for Him, I continued to wait for and pursue the promised full victory.

> "...the LORD will be a shelter for His people,
> and the strength of the children of Israel."
>
> Joel 3:16

Me with my mom, Gertrude.

Chapter Ten

RESTORE TO
YOU THE YEARS

Several years passed, and I was in the midst of planning another short visit home when a young woman, a fellow Bible college student, approached me, saying, "I've been praying for you and feel the Lord has spoken to me that He will be doing a healing work between you and your father on this particular trip."

What? How could she know there was even an issue? I had not revealed this personal and private information to her.

She lingered, looking at me intently and hoping to receive confirmation from me that this was a legitimate need and an appropriate dispatching of what she had heard from the Lord. Although I had been praying relentlessly regarding this desire of my heart, I was a bit stunned that the Lord was giving me such a definite time and explicit description of His plans through an individual who I did not yet possess a trusted and tried friendship.

Finally, I was able to speak. "Oh, thank you for sharing that with me. Yes, I will join my faith with yours that this is the time for that work to take place."

More hopeful than ever, and with this personal word of promise tucked securely in my heart, I flew home.

The five days allotted for my visit (my new, personal boundary) passed quickly, and before I knew it, it was time to go back to the airport. Nothing had happened. Where was the fulfillment of the promise? Had this woman been mistaken? Had I misinterpreted something?

Painful memories were rushing through my mind as I felt bewildered and disappointed. Memories I had hoped would be erased by healing. Distraught, I picked up my suitcase and said my usual verbal goodbyes to my parents and three brothers still living at home. No hugs or good-bye kisses were given or received. After all, my family had never expressed love in that pure manner.

"Stop. Turn around and go back. Tell your father you love him and kiss him on the cheek."

Frozen in place, my mind was whirling. I had heard that voice before, but this time, it was so loud, I wondered if my brothers had heard it, too.

I knew I had to obey. Though my rationale provided a host of reasons why I should not or could not, my spirit within and the presence of God all around me simultaneously cancelled out those thoughts.

As I turned and did all I had been instructed to, I felt the invisible, but very real walls that had divided my father and me for years crumble to dust. The final vestiges of emotional, mental, and physical trauma, and of rejection and heartbreak were being miraculously cleansed away. Within seconds, the stabbing pain from his last words spoken to me before I left for Bible college were erased. The violent acts my father committed against my mother and my siblings were forgiven. Deep-seated anger I had suppressed because he had not protected me from sexual molestation by a family member was uprooted and removed from me.

Had there been a great chasm between us? Had there been impenetrable walls of pain, rejection, misunderstanding, and mistrust? They were sovereignly demolished in a matter of seconds. God had just done the impossible! He had restored the relationship between my father and me. He had fulfilled the promise voiced to me in Seattle.

From that moment forward, I knew that I was accepted back into my family, and that I was being catapulted into a season of healing from the life-altering wounds of wrong and impure actions perpetrated upon me. And I knew a season of healing was coming for every member of my family! We had all suffered, my father and mother included, but our God had demonstrated His desire and His power to heal the unhealable, to solve the unsolvable, and to restore the unrestorable!

I'll try this again, I thought. Picking up my suitcase for the second time and heading toward the car that would transport me to the airport, I glanced back for my final wave goodbye. What I saw next will never be forgotten.

My father was standing within the makeshift screened porch attached to our mobile home, waving goodbye, tears running down his face. This was the first time in my life I had ever seen such a display of pure love and emotion come from him. Once again, God's handiwork of extravagant love took my breath away!

From that day on, we enjoyed pleasant family visits and conversations, whether in person or over the phone. God's word to me had been fulfilled. I had both witnessed and been a participant in another miracle—a miracle of restored love, trust, true safety, and peace.

> "So I will restore to you the years that the swarming locust has eaten, the crawling locust, the consuming locust, and the chewing locust . . . you shall eat in plenty and be satisfied, and praise the name of the LORD your God, who has dealt wondrously

with you; and My people shall never be put to shame."

Joel 2:25–26

My dad and I share a special moment.

Chapter Eleven

MY DELIVERER

It was my second year of Bible college, and I was attending a retreat for single women. With a specific focus on overcoming self-hatred, the leaders had asked us to repeat after them the simple phrase, "I am beautiful."

How could they ask me to lie to myself? I questioned. *I can't say that.* The instruction was repeated. *Why don't they just move on to something else? I can't do this. I am not beautiful. In fact, I'm ugly, and besides my own, I have plenty of opinions from others to confirm and substantiate that.*

The spoken focus of this retreat had launched me back in time to painful elementary and high school encounters. As is so common in our preteen and teenage years, I had not escaped having classmates who described me with hurtful words that had crushed and almost eradicated my self-esteem. I had often been the butt of jokes and had felt the disdain of my peers. Certainly, my home situation had exposed me to much ridicule and rejection.

My journey down this unpleasant memory lane was interrupted by the leader's next question: "How many of you had difficulty repeating that statement? Please raise your hand."

Reluctantly, my hand went up in the air, though my mind was furiously racing with defensive thoughts ranging from *this is just another chance to be embarrassed* to *perhaps someone will come and pray for me since my case is so severe.*

"Now then, those of you with your hands raised, I want you to turn around and kneel right where you are. No one is going to come and pray with you; this is between you and the Lord. You pray, and He will set you free from whatever bondage keeps you from being able to accept and voice the truth of how truly beautiful you are."

Feeling critical and agitated, I thought to myself, *Fantastic. Nobody's going to help. Well, I question the wisdom of that instruction.*

Everyone else was doing it, so I yielded, as well. My knees had barely hit the floor when I was suddenly catapulted into a vision experience so real that my body began to shake. Standing before me was an ominous dark creature with a mirror in his hand. He towered above me and seemed to gloat in the greatness of his stature. There was no mistaking this being: it was demonic, and it was intent on hurting me as much as it possibly could.

The mirror in its hand was cracked and revealed a grotesque distortion of my face and entire body. Reverberating through the atmosphere and filled with other-worldly hatred came the words, "This is what you look like!"

Quickly, I turned away. I could look at it no longer. "Jesus," I called, "Where are you? Why have you left me here to face this dark figure alone?"

Still shaking, I continued to cry out to the Lord.

"Jesus, why haven't you come to deal with this enemy? I feel as though he will take my life. Deliver me!"

If I prayed this audibly or even moved my lips, I cannot say. Everything else had faded away and there was nothing in this place, but me and it. Surely, I would perish unless someone more powerful rescued me.

As this vision experience continued, my focus shifted, and I saw movement out of the corner of my eye.

"It's Jesus! He's come! I am so relieved. Why is He just standing there? He needs to engage and conquer this enemy. Come, Jesus; please come."

But there was no advancement, no engagement. Jesus remained where I first saw Him. Finally, He took one step forward and I could see that He also held a mirror. He spoke one word only.

"*Choose.*"

"Choose? Choose what? What do you mean, Jesus?" This didn't exactly seem the time for casual and enigmatic conversation.

I watched as Jesus positioned His mirror so that my face was reflected in it. Again, the one-word instruction came.

"*Choose.*"

Finally, I understood that by choosing to see myself in Jesus' mirror rather than the enemy's, I would see my true beauty and self-hatred would be overcome.

"I choose Your mirror, Jesus."

With this decision of my will, the ominous force disappeared like a puff of smoke. Jesus and I exchanged smiles, the vision experience ended, and I was suddenly back in the room of the retreat center, aware of everything around me.

Although self-hatred had me by the throat, choking out life daily, Jesus entered the scene and had been my Deliverer once again. He had just dramatically demonstrated to me how easy it was for Him and how great His power was to overcome demonic forces that wanted me to believe they had the potential to destroy my life. If He had done that with self-hatred, He could do it with anything and everything else.

My confidence in and my dependence upon Him continued to flourish. He was making me new through His unconditional and unstoppable love and power. My personal life seemed to be calming down a bit, and I could only wonder what would come next.

> "Then I called upon the name of the LORD:
> O LORD, I implore You, deliver my soul!"
>
> Psalm 116:4

Chapter Twelve

HONOR YOUR FATHER AND MOTHER

If ever there is a day I need things to go well, it is today!

Fighting off nervousness, I sat with hundreds of hopeful applicants waiting for my turn to be called into a makeshift interview station within a well-known delivery company's warehouse.

When my number was announced, I navigated my way between the rows of folding chairs in the waiting area and sat down across from my interviewer. He was dressed semi-casually in a crisp white shirt and pleated khaki slacks. He began with introductions and a brief welcome while I prayed that my answers to his questions would be well-articulated and my presentation professional.

From the time of my initial move to Washington State in 1977, I had worked a variety of jobs. Some of those did not afford the opportunity to fully capitalize on my high school training and my bent toward administrative work.

I loved typing, shorthand and accounting. Details, figures, accuracy, and excellence in all things mattered to me. Perhaps growing up in a chaotic home environment had fueled my deep-seated need for order.

Employed first as a fast-food server in a department store, then as a member of the laundry services staff in a local hotel, my wages were sufficient for survival, and I reminded myself daily to be thankful that I was employed and that my basic needs were met. Still, I longed for a greater opportunity to use the skills and talents that more closely aligned with my desired field of secretarial or administrative support.

This job opening for a cashier/clerk was the perfect next step. The bonus was that I would be in a safer work environment than the secluded basement level of a hotel—or so I thought.

During the interview, I struggled to resist being distracted by memories of frightening occasions when I had had to hide from drunken hotel guests who had wandered into the lower-level hotel laundry area by mistake.

Knowing that several of my friends from Bible college worked there afforded me a sense of peace and safety about this potential new work environment. They spoke so confidently that this company could provide not only a job to satisfy my immediate needs, but also good benefits and the hope of a long and successful career.

As the interview progressed, I realized the part-time hours would allow me to continue my full-time Bible college training. The wages would not only cover basic living expenses, but I would have some discretionary dollars, as well.

My mind was racing with excitement at the prospect of what could be, yet right in the middle of the interview, one specific promise dropped into my thoughts: if I would honor my father and mother, it would go well with me in my new land.

Though so many aspects of our family life had been horribly wrong, I knew this promise from the Scriptures still applied and that it applied in this immediate moment. If I would forgive my father and choose to find every possible way to honor my parents, I would experience God's good hand of favor upon my life. I knew I needed the favor of the Lord. I needed Him to touch my interviewer's heart and mind so that all might go well with me.

Silently, I breathed out a prayer: "It's time, Jesus. It's time for me to choose to let go of the past. Just as you forgave me all my sins, I forgive my father. I forgive my mother. I know she did everything she possibly could to protect me, but was so beaten down herself she was incapable of doing more. I choose to honor my parents in word and in deed. Help me to live with this understanding and practice this principle from Your Word for the rest of my life. Jesus, may my interviewer select me from among the hundreds who are as qualified as me for this open position."

Before the interview concluded, I was offered a part-time job and my starting date was determined. Heaven had heard my cries, including the silent, last-minute ones! God had been faithful to His Word again. Now, I needed to be faithful, too. To look for every possible avenue, no matter how insignificant it seemed, to extend respect and honor to those who had given me life.

My exciting new position primarily involved handling cash and checks received for delivered packages, but it also afforded valuable training in personal interactions. I was learning to serve and support the employees, specifically the delivery drivers, through our daily business interactions and general conversation.

As I hoped, the work environment was very enjoyable. Generally speaking, it was safer, as well. I looked forward to going to my job, to seeing my new friends, and to having my account sheet balance every night. Everything was going along so well…

Then one peculiar evening, I noticed a young man approaching my cashier's window. Though this often happened with employees seeking to change dollar bills into coins for the vending machines, this time I sensed an alarm in my being. Something was very wrong with this scenario. His manner of dress did not coincide with the temperature inside our warehouse. We were dressed in long sleeves because fall was approaching, but he wore a heavy wool coat more appropriate for late January weather. Besides, it was far too late into the evening for any of my regulars to approach me for change.

"Put all of the cash into this brown bag," he said as he pointed a gun at me. An old paper bag was then shoved through the small glass opening of my workstation.

Slowly, I turned my body toward the inner vault where I had just dropped and locked up the intake for that day. As I lifted the money out and began to stuff the bag, I silently began to pray for the Lord to protect me. In His favor and goodness, He had blessed me with this job, now I needed Him to shield me!

In that moment of crisis, I decided that once I had handed off the money, I would duck behind the counter and pray that he didn't reach in and shoot me. Within seconds, everything had transpired, and I crouched, frightened but unharmed, under my counter. I do not know how many anxious minutes passed before shock gave way to common sense and it occurred to me that I probably should inform someone of what had just happened. Trusting Jesus that it was safe for me to stand up and leave my station to find help, I reached out to a co-worker stationed only twenty feet away from me.

He was able to call the police on my behalf and the investigation process was set in motion.

Not until the responding officer's report had been taken and the incident relived did the gravity of the situation begin to sink in. I had just been divinely protected from bodily harm and potentially death, but how would my employer handle the situation? Though other people had been nearby, had anyone seen or heard anything that transpired? Would my employer trust that I was telling the truth? Would I lose my job?

Fortunately, I had been blessed with a supervisor who trusted and respected me, and my job was safe. Additional security measures were put into place, and work went back to normal.

This traumatic experience had shown me, yet again, that my Heavenly Father was truly watching over and protecting me.

In the following years, I held several other jobs, still searching for that perfect fit. Though I had not yet met them, I would shortly become a member of an excellent team of people who the Lord would use to teach me so much more about compassion, and the true meaning of servant leadership.

With so much favor in my everyday life, with Jesus helping me to forgive and choose to honor my parents and His protection over me during a robbery at gunpoint, I struggled to admit that there was still a layer of loneliness inside of me; a deep ache and sense of unfulfillment. How would the Lord Jesus resolve that? What did He have in store for me?

> "Honor your father and your mother, as the LORD your God has commanded you, that your days may be long, and that it may be well with you in the land which the LORD your God is giving you."
>
> Deuteronomy 5:16

Chapter Thirteen

SEEK FIRST
THE KINGDOM

Bible college had often been nicknamed "bridal college." Indeed, many met as fellow students or church members and married, and it would be no different for me. Deep within, I knew there was much to be done to prepare me for that blessing.

As a single woman, a perpetual item on my prayer list had been that Jesus would help me to become the wife my husband would need me to be. I asked the Lord daily to transform me, mature my character, and cause me to become more like Him. I longed to be a woman who would match the description of the virtuous wife found in Proverbs 31:10–12. "Who can find a virtuous wife? For her worth is far above rubies. The heart of her husband safely trusts her; so he will have no lack of gain. She does him good and not evil all the days of her life."

Years passed, and I watched my closest friends, Carol and Connie, find their perfect match and marry. When would it be my turn? Though I'd begun praying in my late teens, I would have to wait until I was thirty years old before my happy day would come.

During those years, which at times seemed like an eternity, I experienced some personal transformations that surprised me. More precious than anything was that of being given a heart to be a stepmother.

***

Several times, I had been asked to teach Sunday school, but had declined to do so. Being the last born in my own family, I had not had opportunities or experience with young children, and quite frankly, I was frightened by this unknown area of life. That would change dramatically.

As I entered church one day, I came upon a young child standing in the middle aisle of the main sanctuary. So firm was his stance that it seemed he had been positioned there to intercept me. He did not speak at all, nor did he move to let me pass by. How awkward this encounter seemed. Seconds passed and I became aware of the presence of the Lord surrounding both of us. I gazed into his eyes that appeared full of light, almost angelic.

Something began happening inside of me. I could feel a softening taking place, almost like hardened wax melting.

Finally, noticing his shoes were untied, I knelt down in front of him.

"Would you like me to help you tie your shoes?"

With a slight nod of his head and eyes twinkling, he consented. I tied his shoes and he quickly moved around me and ran out of view.

When I stood up, I realized I had just experienced another unexpected encounter from God. This one too was a significant and life-changing transformation.

A huge deposit of the love of God for children had just been placed into the bank of my heart. *I'm going to say yes the next time they ask me to teach Sunday school,* I thought to myself. *In fact, I'm not going to wait for them to ask me again; I think I'll go volunteer right now.*

This sweet miracle of becoming one who loves children was a necessary component in my preparation for marriage for it would not be long afterward that I would meet the man of my dreams—a man with two sons.

Equally as important in my growth process was the complete change in my way of thinking about physical expressions of love. How could I marry any man when I had so many hideous memories of impure expression, lack of expression, molestation, and sexual abuse seeking to block me from receiving the blessings that should rightfully proceed from pure love? Would I even be able to have a safe and pleasurable physical relationship with a spouse?

> "But seek first the kingdom of God and His righteousness, and all these things shall be added to you."
>
> Matthew 6:33

My second grade Sunday school classroom.

Chapter Fourteen

ALL THINGS ARE POSSIBLE

Years went by and I continued to pray for help, guidance, and clear direction on how to prepare for a healthy marriage. I studied the Holy Scriptures on this topic, read books, sought counseling, and submitted myself to times of prayer for personal healing and restoration.

I reflected on how blessed others were who had grown up in loving homes with parents who modeled true love and care for each other. What a valuable head start it gave them toward building their own successful relationship.

Needless to say, this heritage was not afforded to me or my siblings. Sadly, it had not been afforded to my parents either. I slowly realized they could not wholly instill in us what they did not themselves possess.

One thing I knew for sure was that I would never marry a man given to alcohol. Beyond that, I had a profound realization that if I did not obtain the next level of personal healing I needed, it would be grossly unfair to the one committing himself to me for life.

My personal preparation would have to include more trips down memory lane; a lane I would have preferred to never traverse again. I would have to be willing to examine the underlying reasons and causes that had brought me to my current state of being before I could progress on into mature healing.

Ready or not, I had learned enough of God's goodness to know He would give me all the strength and grace I needed for this process. Thus, I entered a season that included much reflection on the formative years of my life, going all the way back to the real-life story of how my parents first met and how our family came to be.

***

Born in rural Illinois in 1914 and 1920 respectively, my father and mother dated, fell in love, and married on Valentine's Day in 1939.

Not unlike many in that generation who were needed to work the farm or to otherwise help provide financial support for their struggling families, their formal education had not gone beyond the sixth grade. Still, both possessed a common sense intelligence, sincere religious faith, strong work ethic, and deep love for the children born to them.

The early years of their marriage, I was told by my siblings, were filled with more pleasant happenings than the scant ones etched into my memory bank.

My mom, Gertrude, loved living in the rural areas. She cherished her freedom to be outdoors, take walks, sit in the sun on a hillside, garden, fish, and pick blackberries. She knew the name of every snake and which mushrooms were safe for us to eat. Yet, nothing garnered more of her passion than her children. We were her life.

She was always sticking up for us. She never spanked us and would do anything to keep us safe. Mom worked miracles to keep us clothed and fed. She preserved vegetables, fruits, and rabbit meat to feed us during the winter months. She made the best homemade bread, blackberry pie, and gravy for every breakfast. If one of us was sent to bed with no supper, she would sneak a biscuit or a piece of chicken to us.

My mother never worked outside our home, never obtained a driver's license, never traveled by air, and never went beyond the Illinois state borders. Yet this legacy remains: she did everything in her power to love, care for, and keep her children safe.

My dad, Leo, loved music and dancing. He was fond of taking my mother, all "dolled up" with her long hair flowing, to the local tavern where he would busy himself playing the violin and accordion and they would "cut the rug" in the current dance style.

My sister, Barbara, told me once, "As children, we waited for mom to arrive home in her gray tweed coat. We knew she would have Juicy Fruit gum and chocolate bars hidden for us in her pockets."

Dad worked hard at farming, at sawmills, steel mills, and on the railroads. I was told by my siblings that it was during the latter profession that things began to go horribly awry. Drinking became a daily occurrence during the railroad years, and soon, its death-grip was manifest in my father's life in many abuse-filled ways.

More than once, while my mother was going into labor with yet another child, my father was absent from home and my brothers and sisters did not know how or where to reach him. The outbursts of rage and physical, emotional, and mental abuse led to my mother having three nervous breakdowns and being institutionalized twice. Countless times, my sisters or brothers would have to step into the middle of physical fights to keep her safe.

My siblings were not exempt from the alcohol-driven physical abuse. They were slapped, hit, thrown down stairways, assaulted with pieces of wood, and threatened with knives and a rifle.

The normal parameters of pure love and of physical, mental, and emotional care that healthy families experience were almost nonexistent for us. Consequently, through more than one individual, many members of my family were subjected to sexual abuse and molestations too vile to be described.

***

With this as my heritage, how could I possibly be free? How could I hope for a safe, trusting, and happy marital relationship? It seemed impossible, but by then, I had learned to hold onto the promises of God's Word. Even the ones that seemed like "pie in the sky."

One decision, one healing, one deliverance, one step at a time, I experienced the fulfillment of what is testified of Jesus in 1 John 3:8, "... For this purpose the Son of God was manifested, that He might destroy the works of the devil."

Jesus was teaching me that He had the power and the willingness to heal me of all the destructive works that had taken place in my life. So great was His extravagant love for me that nothing of evil needed to remain to hold me in bondage or torment—not even the pain entrenched in memories.

During this healing season of my life, I was also being taught that this was a two-pronged process. I was receiving abundantly from the loving hand of God. I was being renewed and given hope for a bright and prosperous future. But what about those who had been the perpetrators of the abuse and torment?

Bible verses regarding forgiving those who have sinned against us were being written on my heart. Perhaps the most powerful of all was what is universally called "the Lord's Prayer." In the Amplified Bible, Luke 11:4 reads like this, "And forgive us our sins, for we ourselves also forgive everyone who is indebted to us [who has offended or wronged us]. And lead us not into temptation [but rescue us from evil]."

This verse as well as the parable of the unforgiving servant in Matthew chapter 18 became guideposts for me during this particular part of my Christian journey and growth. Yes, I was being healed, but I also needed to forgive everyone who had offended and wronged me. Jesus had already revealed to me the importance of forgiving and honoring my parents, but I knew He was calling me to extend this forgiveness to others who had also preyed upon me during my teenage years.

As I extended forgiveness to my offenders, it seemed I was no longer enjoying a river of healing waters, but now I had been launched into the ocean! Wave after wave of healing rolled over me! I was truly being transformed in the most vulnerable of areas once so raw with savage pain, grief, anger, and shame.

I was experiencing what must have been a taste of the decree of our Heavenly Father in Revelation 21:5, "Then He who sat on the throne said, 'Behold, I make all things new.' And He said to me, 'Write, for these words are true and faithful.'"

My best friend and my God had heard my cries and answered them beyond anything I would have dreamed possible. I may not have felt completely ready for the major step of marriage, but I knew a tremendous volume of preparation had taken place!

"I'm thirty years old. Now is it time for that special one to come into my life?"

> "But Jesus looked at them and said, 'With men *it is* impossible, but not with God; for with God all things are possible.'"
>
> Mark 10:27

Mom and Dad with my brother, Louis, and sister, Joanna.

Chapter Fifteen

DESIRES OF MY HEART

Song lyrics commonly remain in our memory, but some are etched on our heart, as well. Such were the words to a beloved song, "It's Your Sweetness," written by a dear friend and sung to me on August 4, 1990.

Locking my gaze with my soon-to-be husband, guitar in his hands, his lips close to the microphone, I slowly walked forward as he sang me down the aisle. I could barely keep the tears from gushing and removing all of my professionally applied bridal makeup.

His voice quavered with emotion at times, but the lyrics were resonating throughout my entire being as he sang, "It's your sweetness; it's your love that satisfies."

Had the Lord Jesus really granted to me this greatest of all blessings that I should be able to marry the man of my dreams? Wasn't this just fairy-tale material? It was not, and my heart was pricked that I should stop asking that question and start verbalizing that I was loved by God as His child; I was one He longed to bless beyond words.

My groom singing me down the aisle.

This was another demonstration of the limitless love of God that was, once again, being poured out from heaven above. I really was walking down that aisle, and that really was him singing to me. We had met at church and established a deep friendship upon which we were now about to build this lifelong covenant of marriage.

Though this day was divine indeed, the months and years leading up to it had not been as carefree or happy. We had each walked our road of testing and trials, of loving and being loved, of being in relationships we thought would be or potentially could be "the one" till the end of time. We had each been refined in the fires that were burning away self-centeredness and teaching us to love others more than we loved ourselves.

I had dated and fallen in love more than once over the course of my years at the Bible college. I had even begun premarital counseling with one longtime boyfriend. However, we were barely two or three sessions into our counseling before we were advised that we were not compatible and should seriously reevaluate whether pursuing marriage was a wise choice for us.

The years following that breakup were perhaps some of the most confusing and challenging for me, but looking back now, I can see how extremely valuable they were in my preparation for a marriage covenant that would endure.

Tony had walked a different road than I, but he, too, had done his time in the refiner's fire that purifies and matures.

From a distance, I had been carefully observing him to see how he responded to life's difficulties—especially times of deep emotional distress and pain. Would he harden his heart toward God? Would he remain steadfast in his commitment to surrender all of his life to Jesus? How would he weather the perfect storm raging in his life? Would he lash out in angry verbal attacks?

I had been raised with a model of marriage that involved extensive abuse. By age thirteen, I had vowed never to marry a man who drank. I had determined never to put myself into a situation where emotional, verbal, or physical assault were common. I had set my standards quite high, and I was not willing to lower them.

Life had taught me enough to know that when we are being tested to the very core of our human makeup, every bit of dross is revealed, and so is the gold that remains when the refining process is over. I was looking for gold.

By the time our wedding day arrived, I had become absolutely comfortable with the belief and trust that, come what may, Tony would abandon neither his commitment to nor his reliance upon Jesus for help and ultimate victory, even in what seemed to be the most devastating of situations. It had become clear to me that he was my pot of gold at the end of the rainbow. I did not deserve him, but I loved him more than words could express.

In marrying Tony, I stepped into the role of wife and stepmother to two wonderful sons.

Though keenly aware that I had been made ready for this day through years of prayers and life experiences, I felt the increased dependence upon God and His Word to help me fulfill these precious roles and accompanying responsibilities.

Nonetheless, there remained one final factor or crucial element that needed to be concretely in place before I could unreservedly say "I do." That element was the reassurance that I would be loved for who I was, not for what a partner wanted to change me into.

As our wedding vows were exchanged, Tony spoke these life-giving words to me. "I promise to love you for exactly who you are, with no intentions or expectations that you become someone else. I promise to always love you for who you are. I desire to love you as Christ does the church."

Not once, but twice, Tony publicly vowed to love me as I was and to not attempt to remake me. That vow opened the door for me to walk into the fullness of knowing my true worth and value not only to Tony, but to the God Who we both loved and served.

Jesus loves the church with an unconditional love and tells us that we are accepted in Him. On my wedding day, I experienced a measure of that love that liberated me and placed me on a foundation that could not be removed. I was loved, and I was accepted for who I was.

How delightful and powerful those vows were. Surely life and death are in the power of the tongue, and I had just been given glorious life and liberty.

True to His promise, Jesus had fulfilled His word and given me the desires of my heart. He had also given me the key to fulfilling my purpose and destiny—His unconditional acceptance.

More than thirty years have passed, and still I know I am most blessed among women. Not only am I loved and cherished by a wonderful, godly man, but I am privileged to be married to one who has kept and will keep his vows to me, and to the Lord Jesus. I am also privileged to be called stepmom by two of the most incredible young men I know on Earth.

My prayer was to become a Proverbs 31 woman, and Jesus has blessed and favored me to be married to the kind of man who exemplifies verse 23 of that same chapter: "Her husband is known in the gates, when he sits among the elders of the land."

Having the support of a spouse who vowed to never stand in the way of me pursuing all I am destined to become is exhilarating. Tony's unselfish love and encouragement launched me into an ocean of endless possibilities for growth. I was free to discover who Irene was, and to continue unhindered in my pursuit of becoming like Jesus and learning to represent Him well.

A new door had opened before me, but I did not yet understand all that lay ahead and how my Heavenly Father would lavish His love upon me not only through Tony, but through so many others who would encourage me to become all that I ever dreamed.

"Delight yourself also in the Lord, and He will give you the desires *and* secret petitions of your heart."

Psalm 37:4 (AMPC)

A family Christmas—Tony, Irene, Kevin and Robert.

Chapter Sixteen

THIS IS THE WAY, WALK IN IT

"See that couple over there? I think you should go introduce yourselves to them." A dear friend had tapped Tony and me on the shoulder to share with us her impression regarding a man and woman who were visiting the church we were attending at that time. This was all the confirmation we needed for we were already quite drawn to them and had purposed to meet them as soon as the service ended.

Hanging onto their car door as they tried to leave the parking lot, we were still conversing about the things of God, realizing how much we shared common vision, especially with regards to our desire to serve and glorify Christ in every way possible. Excitedly, we set a lunch date with them.

Jeff and Donna had just moved to Seattle, Washington from Portland, Oregon. Our initial contact with them was that rare and special occurrence of meeting a stranger, but feeling like you've known them all your life.

Another display of God's extravagant love was unfolding. I was about to experience what it was like to have not only natural parents, but a spiritual father and mother figure in my life who would love me unconditionally and provide a level of care and guidance I never dreamed possible.

***

The decision I had made on that day in 1973 had launched me into a world of life-giving access to a personal relationship with the God of the Bible. I had become a disciple of the greatest and most powerful Teacher in all the world, and I was continually learning, and flourishing in my direct one-on-one relationship with Him.

But now it was time to pursue more comprehensive training to fulfill my greatest life dream—that of becoming a minister of the Gospel of Jesus Christ. This was my destiny and I had sensed it from that first moment I began my walk with Jesus.

I had attended Bible college from 1977 to 1982 and graduated with a Bachelor of Theology Degree. During those years, I sat in classes of systematic Bible teaching Monday through Friday, attended and participated in morning chapel services, learned to give my testimony from the pulpit, learned how to teach and lead women's Bible studies as well as how to teach children the amazing stories and the truth of the Bible. I joined prayer groups and learned how to speak with and listen to my Heavenly Father. My head was filled with Bible knowledge, I had wonderful opportunities for hands-on training, and a solid foundation had been laid in my life.

The time had come for the next phase of training—true mentorship.

Like one graduating from college and entering their field of work, I was about to enter the field of ministry and I needed to be in relationship with those I could trust to help me navigate through the journey. Mentors who would lovingly support me, push me to excel, help me to see and avoid pitfalls, and, above all, help me to grow closer to the one who had engaged me in His service, Jesus.

It was evident that the Lord had already prepared Jeff and Donna to become my key mentors, but even more so, lifelong friends who Tony and I were united with in vision.

They had been in ministry for over thirty years. They had pastored in several well-established churches and written many revelatory Bible-based training materials. Their knowledge and experience base was impressive, but this is not what drew us to lasting friendship and eventual partnership in ministry with them. Rather, it was the way in which they conducted their everyday life.

They modeled loving and serving Jesus with all their heart, soul, mind, and strength. They loved people and looked for every opportunity to bring hope, healing, restoration, joy, and peace to them by introducing them to salvation through Jesus Christ, and then discipling and teaching them in the ways of God revealed in the Bible.

Wherever Jeff and Donna went, a fresh wind electric with life came and changed atmospheres. They were carriers of something beyond natural motivation, self-discipline, and largeness of heart resulting in good works toward mankind. They were carriers of the glory, the magnificent presence, and power of God!

Our friendship grew quickly, as did our bond in spirit.

They had vast ministerial experience, solid and balanced teaching of the Scriptures, and intense vision for the church of the city to truly be a holy, unified, and powerful entity that would declare the good news of the gospel of the kingdom of God and impact their city and region for good.

Much of what Jeff and Donna taught was both confirmation and deeper-level revelation of truths we had come to understand during our season of training at Bible college. There was also new understanding of the role of the church in a city, of the gifts of the Spirit spoken of in 1 Corinthians chapter 12, and the five-fold ministry gifts given to the church in Ephesians chapter 4: apostles, prophets, evangelists, pastors, and teachers. Biblical church government and ministry through servant leadership was central to their message and was something they not only taught, but lived out.

Jeff and Donna's mentorship, and the years Tony and I served in ministry under them, were the most pivotal of my life. I had sat under many Bible instructors and gifted teachers, and walked with many inspiring friends, but was now living the words recorded in 1 Corinthians 4:15, "For though you might have ten thousand instructors in Christ, yet *you do* not *have* many fathers…" Just as the Apostle Paul held a unique role in the training and establishing of the Corinthians in their faith, Jeff and Donna held that same parenting role in my life.

The countless hours they poured into Tony and me equipped us with valuable wisdom and practical tools we would not otherwise have gained. They offered us the opportunity for on-the-job ministry training, helped us establish safeguards, and inspired us to greater faith, vision, and zeal to fulfill our dream of serving Jesus Christ with all our being.

Of even greater impact is that they believed in us, mistakes and all, and steadfastly loved us.

Tony and I found ourselves being launched into the next phase of ministry preparation under their tutelage.

For the next several years, we worked alongside Jeff and Donna, training and teaching with them, supporting them in itinerant ministry, establishing citywide prayer gatherings, and eventually, building a small local church.

Their role in our lives, their investment into us, was invaluable.

So great was the relational bond between the Apostle Paul and one of his fellow laborers in ministry, Timothy, that he spoke of him as his son. Jeff and Tony shared a similar bond. Jeff often called Tony "his Timothy." God manifested His extravagant love toward us by allowing us to be discipled by this dear couple.

Just like how Jeff and Donna's consistent support was forming much needed confidence in me, this part of my character development was also happening in my place of employment.

My Heavenly Father knew me better than I knew myself. He knew I needed additional help to establish a proper level of self-confidence and boldness. In His great wisdom, He was about to introduce me to another treasured mentor who would be highly effective in helping shore up this weak area.

> "Your ears shall hear a word behind you, saying, 'This *is* the way, walk in it,' whenever you turn to the right hand or whenever you turn to the left."
>
> Isaiah 30:21

Preparing for a ministry trip to Portland, Oregon.
(Left to right: Wyman, Jaci, Irene, Tony, Donna, and Jeff.)

Chapter Seventeen

SERVANT OF ALL

This was not a typical Valentine's Day. On February 14, 1994, I received a blessing from heaven. I began working in a coveted position as administrative support for a state-wide educational program serving children with sensory disabilities.

Feeling inadequate, but so honored to step into this role, I could hardly wait to use the skills I had acquired through the years while also gaining new ones. Far and above that, I knew that I had been placed into a program that I could support with my whole heart.

I had long ago learned that my preparation for full-time ministry was not limited to a Bible college classroom, but was happening in every part of my life.

"Jesus, what will You be teaching me as I fulfill my new role?" I prayed.

Weeks before accepting this position, I became aware of the program director, Nancy, and her reputation as a visionary and highly competent leader. In fact, all the program staff were very highly spoken of, and it took no time whatsoever to discover why.

Through our directors, consultants, and related educational service providers, knowledge and multifaceted support was imparted with the greatest compassion and most sincere care to children from birth to twenty-one and their families. This was, indeed, a special team!

Working with colleagues whose education, work, and life experience, skills and abilities were so far above my own afforded moments of intimidation and fear that I might not be able to rise to the high standard solidly established before I ever joined the team.

These moments of feeling inadequate were short-lived due to the actions and attitudes that were consistently shown from the top down. If the administrative staff stayed late hours to make photocopies of documents that had to be postmarked for express shipping, our director stayed right beside us and delivered the boxes to the drop-off location herself.

This modeling of servant leadership was impacting me just like that everyday displayed by my spiritual mentors, Jeff and Donna. Nancy was well within her right to leave work at the close of the day, but she chose to stay behind, roll up her sleeves, and work with us until every task was complete. Even if that meant staying at the office until midnight.

Time after time, when I lacked confidence or felt unable to learn a new technological skill or successfully complete trainings in leadership or presentation skills, Nancy would be the first to encourage and cheer me on. She believed in me even when I couldn't find the courage to believe in myself.

The above examples are only two of the hundreds that could be told concerning my director and other co-workers who constantly chose to put others before themselves, to do all out of pure love and compassion, and to be servants of all.

We worked hard. We worked as a true team. We rejoiced in each other's achievements. We were family, sharing in celebrations and accomplishments, in trials and hardships, and always pulling together for the highest level of benefit for those we were providing services to. And we were friends. Friends forever.

My years of employment in this position were some of the best years of practical ministry training I could possibly have had. They left an eternal impression in my heart and in my spirit, and I am forever grateful.

In Jesus' great love for me, He had carved out this administrative support position and placed me there so I could become more like Him.

He had blessed me with another mentor, Nancy. Her direction, support, and encouragement were working in me a greater self-confidence that helped me push through to accomplish things I never thought possible. Her modeling of servant-leadership impacted me daily.

It was during this season of growth in my life that I was about to receive some grievous news...

> "And He sat down, called the twelve, and said to them,'If anyone desires to be first, he shall be last of all and servant of all.'"
>
> Mark 9:35

Chapter Eighteen

ALL YOUR HOUSEHOLD WILL BE SAVED

In his eightieth year of life, my father's health was failing quickly due to a diagnosis of cancer.

My mother had been placed in a nursing home the year prior. The years of physical and mental abuse had certainly taken their toll, and now she battled congestive heart failure, adult-onset diabetes, and dementia.

We received a call from my brother Ted saying that we might want to plan a visit to Illinois soon. Quickly, we arranged flights for my husband, my brother Bill, and me. Knowing how much my dad enjoyed music, Tony decided to bring his guitar on the trip.

Upon arrival, we learned that my dad had just come home from the local hospital where he had undergone chemotherapy treatments. A special visitor had been in to see him; the same minister who pastored the church where my brother had received salvation in his teens. Ironically, years before, during an attempted home visit to our family, my

121

father had threatened this minister with a rifle and run him off our property. Compelled by the extraordinary love of Jesus and the desire to share the Gospel with every man and woman, the minister returned to reach out to my father in his final hours.

Though suffering side effects of chemotherapy, my father was able to acknowledge that while in his hospital bed and feeling quite groggy, he had engaged in conversation and prayer with this minister.

Additionally, my dad shared with us a letter he had recently received from his closest neighbor. Placed in the same package as the apple pie she had baked to bless my dad and two brothers still living at home, was a one-page, hand-written letter spelling out the plan of salvation.

Through the mouth of two or three witnesses, something was being established. The atmosphere was being set for my dad's entrance into and acceptance of the good news of the gift of eternal life. Demonstrated through the faithful perseverance of the minister who visited him in the hospital, and the thoughtfulness and loving kindness of his neighbor, the unconditional love of God was relentlessly chasing my father down.

"Play something for me on your guitar, Tony," my dad requested. As Tony began to strum the chords and sing, the atmosphere in my family's single-wide mobile home changed.

Sensing the sweet presence of the Lord, we all became unmistakably aware that this was a God-ordained moment. The promise of Scripture that all my household would be saved was pulsating within me.

When the song finished, we asked my dad if he was certain of his eternal destiny. Did he know, beyond a shadow of a doubt, that when his time on Earth was finished, he would enter heaven to be with Jesus Christ forevermore? His response was one I will never forget.

"I want to, but I don't know how. I think that man in the hospital prayed with me, but I can't recall it clearly."

Tears were streaming down all our faces as we knelt before him. My brother Bill took his hands and led him in a prayer of repentance unto salvation. Never before had I witnessed the magnitude of peace as that which was now visibly settling over his face. It was as though, in addition to his spirit, his whole body had come into release and comfort.

Only weeks later did we receive another phone call. Sitting quietly on the sofa at home, having just finished eating a sandwich for lunch, my dad laid his head back and peacefully slipped into eternity.

The grief of loss came rushing in, but along with it came irrefutable confidence that my father had experienced true transformation. Darkness had lost its hold on him, and the light of God's rich and gracious gift of eternal life had visibly manifested in his eyes. He had become a new creation in Christ Jesus; old things had passed away.

True to His promise given to me in the dream of the serpent of alcoholism ultimately being defeated in my father's life, I was now an eyewitness to that being fully realized. Though our time of tasting the sweetness of that victory on Earth was short, we will have all of eternity to rejoice together in the faithfulness of God to deliver from every bondage.

My father lives now in the presence of Jesus, along with my mother who passed six months later. Surely the truth of the old gospel song "Will the Circle Be Unbroken?" rings out. We will be reunited forevermore with not even a trace of memory of past abuse for all has been washed away through the cleansing power of the blood of Jesus Christ.

The miracle of my father receiving Jesus Christ as his Savior weeks before passing into eternity greatly fueled my desire to be a mouthpiece testifying of the goodness and unconditional love of God.

> ". . . Send men to Joppa, and call for Simon whose surname is Peter, who will tell you words by which you and all your household will be saved."
>
> Acts 11:13–14

Chapter Nineteen

STIR UP THE GIFT

Ordination into the ministry of the Gospel of Jesus Christ had been my deep desire for as long as I could remember. Along with a public proclamation before witnesses on Earth and in the heavens, it was a sober time of dedication and confirmation of calling. It was a powerful time of impartation from heaven of spiritual gifts through the laying on of hands by those who officiated the ordination ceremony.

At the appropriate time, Jeff and Donna, my spiritual parents and the founders of Lion's Roar Ministries and Center of Ministries, publicly recognized the call upon our lives and formally ordained Tony and me as ministers of the Gospel of Jesus Christ.

How grateful and how small I felt during that ceremony. Standing alongside my husband, being ordained into ministry at the very same time, seemed more than I could fully process or grasp. Deep things were transpiring in my spirit; I knew I was being equipped for what lay ahead.

The spiritual gifts spoken of in 1 Corinthians chapter 12 and Romans chapter 12, the very ones I had first seen demonstrated by the Bible college outreach group sent to my rural setting years before, were now being given to me by God.

My mind went back to those silent requests spoken to the Lord when I was in my teens; the requests that one day, I, too, would be prepared and able to help people grow in their personal relationship and walk with Christ.

I recalled how God had appeared to King Solomon and prompted him to ask for whatever he wished to receive. Solomon's request became my own, "… give to Your servant an understanding heart to judge Your people, that I may discern between good and evil…" (1 Kings 3:9).

Scriptures testify that God granted that request and gave Solomon the ability to discern justice and placed within him a wise and understanding heart. What more could I ask for on that day than the heart and wisdom of my Heavenly Father?

My deepest longing was to be able to serve others out of the Shepherd's heart of Jesus Christ Who was not willing to let even one perish.

My lifelong mission was being solidified: to do justly, to love mercy, and to walk humbly with my God. Jesus testified of Himself that He had not come to be served, but to serve. On that memorable day in 1996, I pledged to operate with that same attitude of service.

Quite often, people are asked to sum up in one sentence what they learned from a training in which they have participated or to expound on a life lesson that has profoundly impacted them. During the ordination ceremony, I reflected on the years leading up to this day and realized that my answer to that question would have to be the words continually rehearsed by one of my favorite Bible college teachers: "Ministry is an outflow of your personal relationship with Jesus Christ."

The Apostle Paul stated in the Book of Corinthians that he could do no other thing but preach the gospel or good news of Jesus. His life had been so utterly transformed and he had been so captivated by the unspeakable love of God that he would give his all in response to that love. Surely, I could do no less.

By that point in my Christian life, I had come to realize there was no greater passion than that of representing the character, ways, and works of the God Who had so completely captivated my heart. I had willingly become a bondservant of Jesus Christ. I was entering a new chapter of my life and had been given a license, literally and spiritually, to share my greatest love.

***

I am eternally grateful that a solid foundation was laid for me through all of the men and women of God who faithfully taught me, prayed for me, and supported me in every way possible, especially during my twenties and thirties, but also to this day.

There are not words enough to say how blessed was the day when Jeff and Donna came into our lives. They have both gone before us into the presence of the Lord, but the imprint they left upon our lives is permanent and bears fruit even now. Great is their reward in heaven for Jesus has been able to say to them, *"Well done, my good and faithful servants."*

Whether encouraging one awaiting his fate on death row or speaking to hundreds in conference settings at home or abroad, God's empowering grace has opened doors that I never fathomed. With every opportunity to share the good news of Jesus Christ, I have seen many saved, baptized in the Holy Spirit, and delivered from oppression. Equipping and training believers to fulfill their calling is a joy to my heart, but nothing delights me more than to hear someone I have ministered to say that they are now walking in closer relationship with Jesus and in their identity as beloved children of God.

God's extravagant love, His mercies that are new to me every morning, His loving-kindness and faithfulness have taken me from a young girl, so shy I could barely speak to my friends, to one who loves to share His goodness and faithfulness with all.

I was raised in deep poverty with no indoor plumbing, no telephone, and often not enough food to satisfy or sustain good health. Fear, depression, and anger had dominated me. Due to shame and self-hatred, I could not hold my head high. Yet, I have been so totally transformed, that now I delight in being a vessel for His service and honor, a valued overcomer in Christ, and a friend of God.

He has removed the spirit of fear that tormented me and has given me the spirit of power, love, and a sound mind. I cannot fail to testify of His wonderful works in my life; should I do so, the very rocks would cry out and glorify His great Name!

> "Therefore I remind you to stir up the gift of God which is in you through the laying on of my hands. For God has not given us a spirit of fear, but of power and of love and of a sound mind."
>
> 2 Timothy 1:6–7

ALL THINGS COME FROM GOD

In the New Testament, the Book of 1 John has often been labeled "the book of love." Certainly, it contains one of the most powerful verses of all time. Chapter 4, verse 19 reads, "We love Him because He first loved us."

The story you have just read is my simple testimony of responding to and loving the One Who first loved me. He sought me out and found me in an old farmhouse in Southern Illinois. He chose to love me first. He has given me everything that I have so that I might give back to Him.

The extravagant love I testify of is the same John testified of in his epistle. It is the same love King David testified of. It is the same unconditional love that the thief dying on the cross next to Jesus was offered and received. It is the same love that was offered to everyone in the Scriptures, to everyone in the world, and especially to you.

As it was with me, this love is offered as a gift. Who are you that you should receive this gift? The one God chose to love first.

Receive His extravagant love!

> "Now therefore, our God, we thank You and praise Your glorious name. But who *am* I, and who *are* my people, that we should be able to offer so willingly as this? For all things *come* from You, and of Your own we have given You."
>
> 1 Chronicles 29:13–14

CPSIA information can be obtained
at www.ICGtesting.com
Printed in the USA
JSHW011151100523
41520JS00004B/19

9 781662 877162